WRITTEN BY

LAURENCE OTTEINHEIMER-MACQUET, RAPAHAELLE BRICE,
MARIE FARRÉ, DOMINIQUE JOLY,
CHRISTINE LAZIER, ODILE LIMOUSIN, GAUD MOREL,
CATHERINE DE SAIRIGNÉ

COVER DESIGN BY

STEPHANIE BLUMENTHAL

TRANSLATED BY

PAULA SCHANILEC

PUBLISHED BY CREATIVE EDUCATION
123 South Broad Street, Mankato, Minnesota 56001
Creative Education is an imprint of The Creative Company

Library of Congress Cataloging-in-Publication Data
[Terre qui nous nourrit. English]
World agriculture / by L. Ottenheimer-Macquet et al;
translated by Paula Schanilec.
(Creative Discoveries)
Includes index.
Summary: Presents a historical perspective, describing how different kinds of foods
from around the world are grown, harvested, and consumed.
ISBN: 0-88682-952-6
1. Agriculture—Juvenile literature.   2. Food—Juvenile literature.
[1. Agriculture.   2. Food.]
I. Otteinheimer-Macquet, Laurence.   II. Schanilec, Paula, trans.   III. Title.   IV. Series.
S519.T4313   1999
630—dc21   97-27524
First edition

2 4 6 8 9 7 5 3 1

WORLD AGRICULTURE

CONTENTS

CREATIVE EDUCATION

For centuries people all over the world have eaten bread. It's one of the most basic foods.

Bread is made from dough—a mixture of flour and water—that is baked in an oven. Unleavened bread (bread without yeast) is flat, like a thick pancake. Dough made with yeast rises, and the loaf bakes high and round.

Each type of wheat has a different head of grain; some heads are bearded, with long, coarse whiskers, and some are not.

Flour is made from grains of wheat.

Wheat, like corn, rye, and rice, is a type of cereal. Cereal crops are plants that have a head of grain on each stem. The grain can be eaten whole or ground up to make flour. A husk protects each grain of wheat, and the seed is found inside.

A grain of wheat cut in half to show the seed

The wheat seed develops by feeding off the grain that surrounds it. Gradually, the seed changes into a small green shoot, with roots that draw nourishment from the soil. Finally, a tall stem emerges above the ground. A heavy golden ear of grain tops each stem, and each ear is made up of 40 to 60 grains.

Farmers plow a field into long, straight furrows to plant wheat. Then they use a harrow to break up the clods of dirt. Now the field is ready for seeding. Years ago, farm workers scattered seed by hand. Today farmers use an automatic seed drill, which plants the seeds much more quickly.

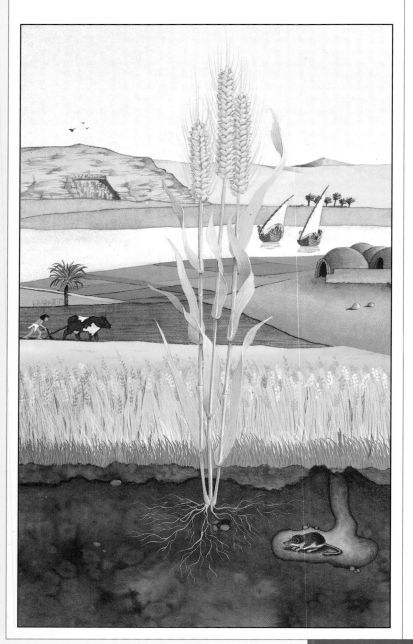

Farmers use plows to create furrows.

Corn dollies were made from stems of wheat. They were hung around the farmhouse to bring good luck.

Now it's time to bring in the harvest. In some countries, workers harvest the wheat by hand. They use sickles to cut the wheat and then tie the crop into bundles called sheaves. The whole village helps to bring in the harvest, and then it's time to celebrate with dances, singing, and, of course, a special harvest supper.

After the wheat is harvested

Years ago, the sheaves were threshed, or beaten, with long, jointed rods called flails. Threshing the sheaves freed the grains from the stalks and ears, which were then kept as straw to feed animals during the winter.

After threshing, workers winnowed the grain to remove hard scales called bracts and to separate the grain from the husks. Workers would use shovels to toss the wheat into the air. The husks were light, so they blew away; the heavier grains fell to

the ground. Another way that workers winnowed grain was to shake it and toss it in a sort of large sieve, called a winnowing basket.

Tiny harvest mice make their nest in the corn stalks.

Workers use sickles to cut wheat; then they tie the wheat into sheaves.

Workers threshed the sheaves with flails and winnowed the pile of grain.

Today combine-harvesters thresh the wheat in one day.

A threshing machine that ran on steam was a rare sight 150 years ago, but what a difference it made to the farmers' work. As workers fed sheaves into the top, the machine separated the grain from the straw.

The modern combine-harvester does the whole job quickly. It cuts the wheat and collects the grain, leaving the straw behind. The grain is fed into a truck that takes it to the farm to be stored.

People used to crush the grain with stones. The Romans invented the millstone—a stone disc that turned on top of another disc to grind grain. A water mill uses the force created by a water current to turn the millstone.

A windmill

If there was no river nearby, people used the force of the wind to drive the sails of a windmill. Both windmills and water mills have a system of interlocking wheels that make the millstones turn. Today's flour mills are automatic and run on electricity.

Bakers prepare the dough with flour and bake bread.

Bakers work through the night so that in the morning there's hot, fresh bread ready to sell. Bakers mix the flour with water, salt, and yeast. A machine kneads together the ingredients to form a firm dough. The bakers shape the dough into balls, weigh them, and leave them in a warm place for several hours. The yeast causes the dough to rise. When the loaves have doubled in size, the bakers lift each one into the oven with a long wooden shovel called a peel.

Bakers weigh each piece of dough and put it in a warm place where it is left to rise.

The oven's heat creates the outside crust. The loaves bake for one or two hours, depending on their size. When the loaves are done, the bakers remove them from the oven, and delicious smells fill the bakery.

Inside an old-fashioned bakery

Loaves come in all shapes and sizes: tall split loaves, squat cottage loaves, or long French sticks. Every country has its own specialty. Bakers working in an industrial bakery make the sliced bread found in grocery stores.

Look closely at a slice of bread and you'll see the tiny holes left by the bubbles of gas during baking.

In different parts of the world, flour is made from other cereal grains.

Many types of flour produce bread. Rye and oats are cereal crops that grow in cold climates. Bread made from rye is dark brown, with a strong, nutty flavor. It is common in Eastern Europe and the Scandinavian countries.

What else are cereal crops used for?

Bakers need flour to make cakes and pastries. Flour may be refined (which is called white flour) or whole grain (which has wheat grains and husks still in it). A North African specialty is **couscous,** made from coarsely ground grains of wheat that are steamed and served with meat and vegetables. **Millet** grows well in Africa too. It is cooked like a porridge or baked as unleavened bread. **Rice** is the most widely grown cereal in Asia.

Maize, or corn, is the main cereal used in South America. Maize flour is made into flat, thin pancakes called tortillas. In Mexico, people eat them like bread. Maize came to Europe in the 16th century, after Christopher Columbus brought it from America.

Paddy rice   Brown rice   White rice

The next time you're eating cereal for breakfast, read the package to see which grain it was made from. The cereal's name may give you a clue.

Once they're dry, maize grains keep all winter.

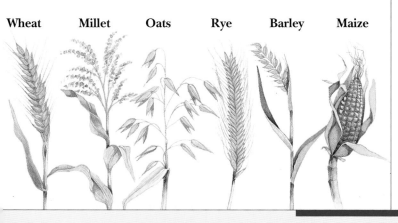

Wheat   Millet   Oats   Rye   Barley   Maize

People from China, India, and other countries in Asia eat rice every day. They may eat a bowl of simple boiled rice, or add meat, fish, or vegetables as well. Rice grows with its roots in water in flooded fields called paddy fields. Rice was one of the first cereal crops that people grew.

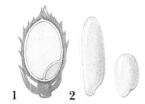

1. A grain of rice cut in half to show its seed
2. Some types of rice have long grains; other types have round grains.

1   2

People eat the kernel of a grain of rice.
Rice plants grow in clumps; each clump produces several ears of grain. As each grain ripens, a fine covering called a husk protects it. The grain contains the seed of the new rice plant and will grow if planted. The stalks of the plant are hollow, so that it can suck up water to feed itself.

For more than 7,000 years, people in China and India have been growing rice.
The methods of growing rice have not changed much in all that time, and people still enjoy eating it. Merchants, soldiers, and sailors brought rice from Asia into the countries they visited. In North America, Native Americans harvested wild rice, which is still popular today.

Many people cook rice by steaming it.

Rice is the staple food for more than half the world's people.

Rice grows best in warm climates.

Today, nine out of every 10 sacks of rice are grown in Asia, and most of it is consumed there. A huge amount of rice is grown in the United States, too, but much of it is sold to the rest of the world.

Herons, wild ducks, frogs, and fish all make their homes in paddy fields—and so do thousands of mosquitoes.

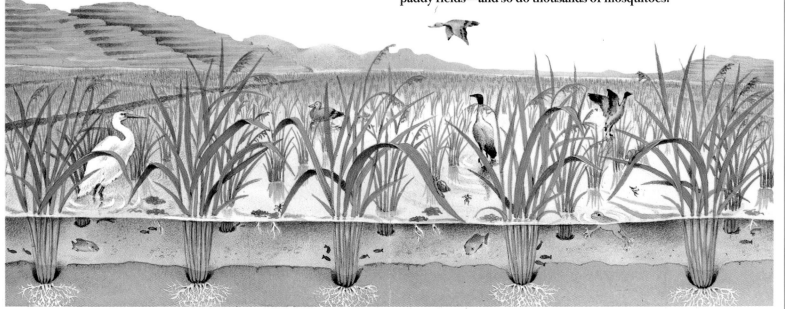

Many hands are needed to look after the paddy fields . . .

To grow rice, workers flood the paddy fields. Ditches carry water from rivers to the fields. Workers raise the low barriers across these ditches to let the water flow into the fields.

After the workers flood the fields, they use plows, harrows, and rollers pulled by buffalo to plow, rake, and flatten the muddy soil. While they finish preparing the paddy fields, another group of workers sow the rice in a separate flooded field called a seedbed.

Next, workers transplant the seedlings. After a month, the young rice plants have grown but are too close together in the seedbed to develop properly. Workers carefully transplant the seedlings to the paddy field—it's hard work. Bent double, ankle deep in water, workers plant the seedlings in straight lines, giving them plenty of space to grow. The water helps keep weeds from growing.

The harvest

Three to six months later, the rice has turned golden, and the heads are heavy with grain. The rice is ripe for harvesting. Just before the harvest, rice growers open the sluice gates in the ditches; the water drains out of the paddy fields back into the river. The mud dries and hardens. From dawn till dusk, rice growers use sickles to cut the stalks, and then they tie the plants into bundles. Other workers carry the crop back to the village.

There, threshers beat the rice stalks against stone rollers to shake off the grain. They stack the stalks and keep them for straw and leave the grain out in the sun to dry. Later, the workers use a mortar with a pestle to crush the loose grain and free the kernels from the husks. Then they winnow the kernels. At this stage, the kernels are brown, whole grain rice. To make white rice, workers must remove the last fine pieces of husk.

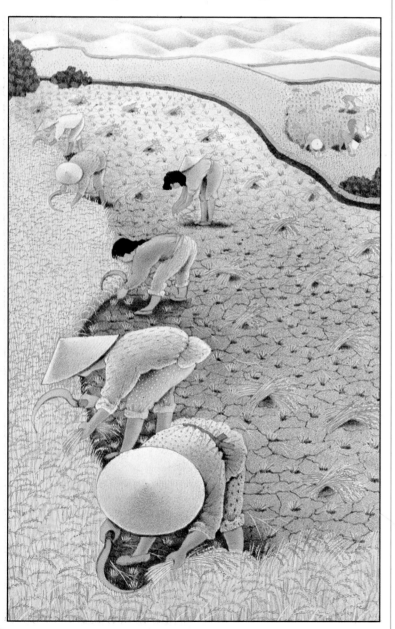

People in Asia use rice in many ways.
Rice growers ferment damaged grains of rice to make beer, or they ground the rice into flour to make cakes and noodles. Some people weave rice straw into baskets and hats. Farmers feed rice husks to their animals or use the husks to make fertilizer. Rice is so important in some countries that farmers build terraces on hills and mountains so that even there rice can be grown in paddy fields. Spring water runs down the terraces in channels.

In the United States, rice is grown in huge fields.

Machines do almost everything. Enormous tractors rake and harrow the rice fields.

Whether on a mountainside or a plain, paddy fields must be level.

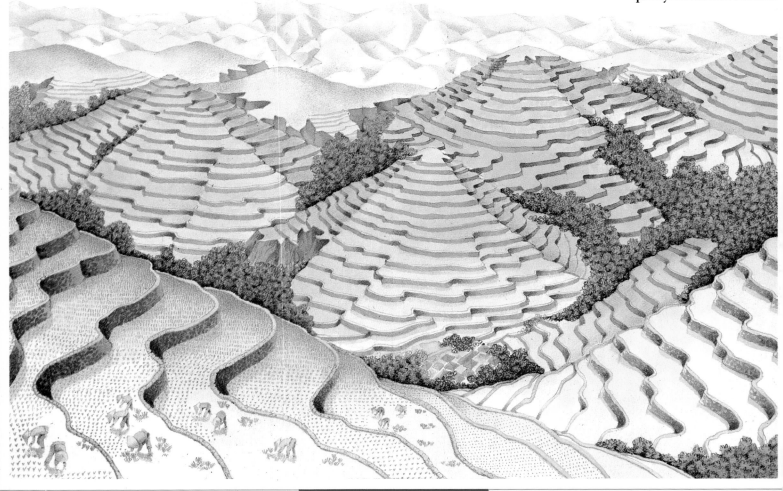

A machine digs channels in the fields. Then water is piped in to flood the channels.

The rice germinates in sacks soaking in water.

Airplanes fly low over the fields to sow the rice seedlings. This method cuts out the need to replant by hand, which involves a lot of costly labor.

Combines gather the ripe plants and automatically separate the straw from the grain. In the factory, the rice is dried, husked, and put into packets.

Rice festivals

In Asia, rice is such an important crop that people organize festivals to ask for a good harvest. Some growers store their rice in special granaries built on stilts to protect the precious contents from floodwaters and hungry animals.

In Europe and North America, people throw rice over newly married couples to bring them good luck.

A granary on the island of Celebes, Indonesia

The word potato is one we have borrowed from the South American Indians who first grew and used the plant. Raw potatoes don't taste very good, but there are many delicious ways of cooking them—including French fries fried in oil until they're crispy and potatoes baked in the oven in their skin.

A potato is a tuber—part of the plant's underground stem that has swollen. Potato plants have a fruit, which looks like a small green tomato. Watch out, though! Potato fruit is poisonous.

If you plant a potato in the soil, you'll end up with 15 to 20 new potatoes. A shoot pushes up through the soil, growing into a stem.

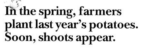

In the spring, farmers plant last year's potatoes. Soon, shoots appear.

The shoot feeds on the nutrients stored in the old potato, which gradually shrivels up as the plant develops. The roots grow and swell into tiny new potatoes. When growing potatoes, farmers heap a small mound of dirt around the base of the plant, because if light gets to the young potatoes, they'll turn green and won't be good to eat.

In the fall, potato plants turn yellow and their leaves wither. These are signals that the potatoes are fully grown and have strong skins. Now it's time to dig up the plants.

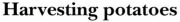

For years, potatoes were harvested by hand.

Harvesting potatoes

Before farm machines were invented, farm workers dug up, or lifted, potatoes with a pitchfork. They would leave the potatoes in the fields to dry and then sort them. The workers kept some as seed potatoes for the next year's crop. They fed damaged potatoes to their animals and kept the rest for eating. For years, however, many people thought that potatoes were a food that only poor people ate. Only in the last 100 years has the potato become popular.

Many different varieties of potatoes are for sale in grocery stores. New potatoes are picked before they are full-grown. Their skins are thin and are hardly a protection for them. They taste delicious, but don't keep for long. Other potatoes store well for up to a year in a dry, dark place, like a cellar. Some types of potato are firm and make good French fries or roast potatoes. Others break down as they cook and are better mashed, baked, or used in soup.

The potato comes from South America. Long ago, the Inca people of Peru in South America found they could grow small potatoes high in the mountains to feed themselves and their animals.

The Spanish discovered the potato when they went to South America. In the middle of the 16th century, General Francisco Pizarro and his soldiers set out from Spain to conquer newly discovered lands. They found the Incas growing a vegetable they called *batata:* the potato. By about 1570, potatoes and other wonders from the New World were arriving by ship in Europe.

The Indians in Peru today, many of them descendants of the Incas, dry their potatoes so that they keep for years. The Indians press out the water, then they leave them outdoors over several nights to freeze.

At first, this vegetable was not popular in Europe. For a long time, European peasants thought the new vegetable would make them ill. They fed potatoes to their pigs rather than eating them, even during years of famine.

Then in the 17th century, a French scientist named André Parmentier had an idea. He set guards around the potato fields, pretending there was something precious growing. Eager to find out what was so special in the field, the peasants crept in at night and stole some potatoes. They soon found out that potatoes were good to eat after all!

On a modern farm, special machines harvest the potatoes.

The machines separate the potatoes from stones and lumps of soil. In the factory, a sorting machine grades the potatoes according to their size. Any that are green or an odd shape are taken out by hand and are not sent for sale. Some potatoes are set aside to make potato powder: first they are boiled, then mashed, and finally dried out in a speical hot-air machine.

Colorado beetle eggs   Larva

The Colorado beetle is the potato's worst enemy. Thirty beetle larvae can devour a whole potato plant in a week. The female beetle lays 2,500 eggs.

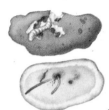

In six weeks, the eggs hatch into larvae, which grow into beetles and lay more eggs. Worms and slugs are pests too. Many farmers spray crops with chemicals to kill bugs and control diseases such as potato blight.

Wasps, gadflies, and ladybugs like to eat the larvae of Colorado beetles.

The different shapes and colors of potatoes

Many different varieties of potatoes exist. All contain vitamins, fiber, and the carbohydrate starch. Purified starch is a white powder. Because it's smooth, absorbent, and gluey, people use starch in sauces, soups, cakes, and ice cream, as well as in glue, cardboard, and even disposable diapers.

Scientists are working to create new varieties of potatoes that can resist disease. They take the pollen from one potato flower and place it carefully on the

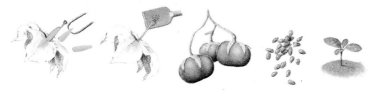

flower of another variety. This is called cross-fertilization.

Scientists keep the new seeds in test tubes and watch the seedlings develop. The scientists move the seedlings to greenhouses until they are strong enough to grow outside.

Growing potatoes in a test tube

Sometimes scientists lift a shoot from a full-grown potato and place it in a test tube on special jelly.

Three weeks later, new shoots have sprouted. These are transplanted in pots. When the leaves and roots appear, scientists divide them into new plants. In this way, two million plants can be grown from a single shoot in less than a year.

Potatoes store well in a cool, dark place.

An apple has pips inside.

A cherry has a pit.

Blackcurrants

Redcurrants

Gooseberries

Strawberries

Raspberries

Fruit comes from the flower of a plant.

Many plants grow flowers that turn into fruits with seeds inside. If they germinate, the seeds grow into new plants. The fruit protects and feeds the seeds as they develop. The seeds of some fruits, like grapes, currants, or melons, are called the pips. The seed of a cherry or plum grows inside a hard shell, called the pit. Raspberries and blackberries are made up of a mass of small fruits all joined together, each with its own pip.

Fresh fruit contains vitamins that are important for our health. Lemons in particular are bursting with vitamin C. In the past, sailors took them on long sea voyages, because without vitamin C, they risked developing a disease called scurvy. A Kiwi fruit has twice as much vitamin C as an orange.

We eat fruit when it's ripe. That is when it is soft and sweet. Some fruits are picked before they have ripened naturally on the tree; bananas are picked while they are green, and they finish ripening on their long journey to market. Fruits like mangoes or litchis, which come from countries with tropical climates, travel in chilled containers; this helps keep the fruit fresh, and kills any insects that might harm them.

Quince

Apricot

Greengage plum

Peach

Pear

Mirabelle plum

Plum

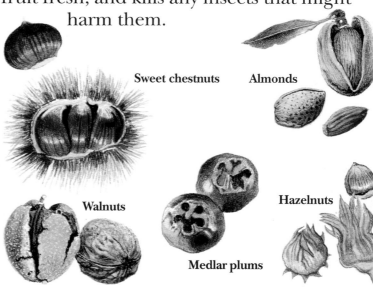

Sweet chestnuts

Almonds

Walnuts

Medlar plums

Hazelnuts

Apples and pears are stored in cool places. This keeps the fruit fresh for several months after it has been picked.

Once it's ripe, fruit must be eaten or stored. Heating fruit is a way of preserving it. When fruit is cooked, the heat sterilizes it, killing the bacteria that make it rot. Sugar also helps to preserve fruit—which is why jam and canned fruit can be kept so long. Heat-treated fruit is also used in ice cream and yogurt. Most fruits can be squeezed and crushed to make juice drinks. **Grape juice can be made into wine.** Grapes are picked in the fall, when they are ripe and full of sugary juice. After they are crushed, the juice ferments and turns into alcohol. It is put in barrels, then bottled, to allow it to age. Apple juice can be made into cider.

Grapes

Watermelon   Melon

Pomegranate

Dates

Lemon

Guavas

Bananas

Orange

Figs

Litchis

Pineapples

Mango

Vegetables are part of our daily diet, whether we eat them raw or cooked, fresh, frozen, or from a can. They are vital for our health because of the many vitamins and minerals they contain.

Vegetables originated from wild plants. Sea cabbage growing on sand dunes, for example, produced cauliflower and broccoli. Over centuries, people learned which wild plants were best to eat. They collected seeds from the strongest plants, sowed them, and developed new varieties.

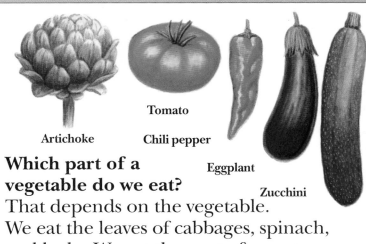

Artichoke   Tomato   Chili pepper   Eggplant   Zucchini

Which part of a vegetable do we eat?

That depends on the vegetable. We eat the leaves of cabbages, spinach, and leeks. We eat the root of carrots, beets, and radishes, but the fruit of tomatoes, eggplant, cucumbers, and zucchini. Have you noticed seeds in those fruits? An onion and a clove of garlic are the bulbs of their plant, and an artichoke is actually a flower. Peas are seeds; beans are seed pods. Brussels sprouts, with their small, tightly packed leaves, are buds.

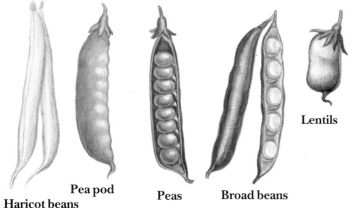

Haricot beans   Pea pod   Peas   Broad beans   Lentils

Do you enjoy homegrown fruits and vegetables? Today, most of the fresh fruits and vegetables we eat have been grown in large fields, harvested by machines, and purchased at grocery stores. Often, this produce has traveled hundreds or even thousands of miles before we eat it.

Some people prefer to grow their own fresh produce on a farm or in a garden plot. Others shop at farmers' markets.

We like to eat a variety of vegetables all year round. But in order to do so, farmers must grow them in greenhouses or in fields under tunnels of plastic that hold the sun's warmth. Asparagus shoots start to grow in the spring. Some are kept covered with soil, and because they don't get light, they grow into long, white stems, tender to eat. Button mushrooms are also grown in the dark to keep them from opening up.

Most vegetables contain fiber. Fiber is needed to help our digestive system work well. Fiber helps food to pass through intestines quickly and efficiently. Lentils, broad beans, kidney beans, cabbage, and spinach are all high in fiber.

Endive

Cauliflower

Brussels sprouts

Cabbage

Lamb's lettuce

Lettuce

Spinach

Sorrel

Leek

Garlic

Shallot

Onion

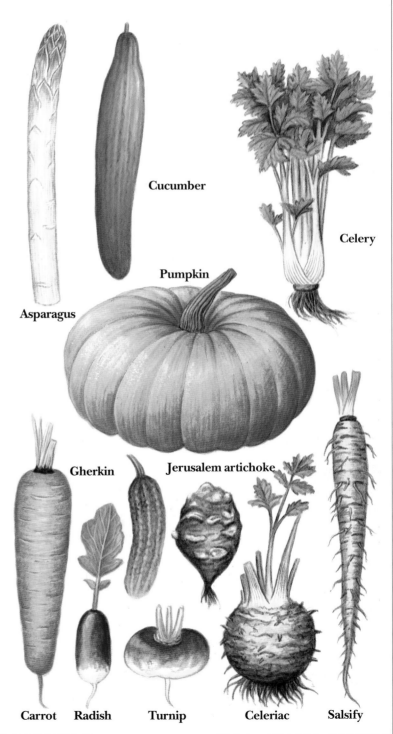

Cucumber

Celery

Pumpkin

Asparagus

Gherkin

Jerusalem artichoke

Carrot

Radish

Turnip

Celeriac

Salsify

Spring is the busiest time of the year. In the spring gardeners sow pea, bean, and carrot seeds and plant potatoes and onions. Gardeners shield radishes and lettuce from the cold by using glass frames or covering the young plants with plastic sheeting until the weather is warmer. They put nets around strawberries and other fruits to protect them from birds that love to feast on the ripe berries.

The warmth of the summer sun helps everything grow. Plants flourish in the sunshine, but so do weeds. Gardeners pull out the weeds so they don't rob flowers and vegetables of sunshine, moisture, and nutrients. In dry periods, gardeners water the beds every evening, when the sun is not so hot. Most vegetables and berries are ready to be picked in the summer.

Each fruit and vegetable has its season.

In fall, the days grow shorter. The nights get colder. It's time to harvest the last of the fruits and vegetables, and, in some climates, plant cool-weather vegetables such as cabbages and leeks. Gardeners hoe manure or garden compost into the soil to put back some of the nourishment the plants used during the year. Some gardeners plant dahlias and chrysanthemums to give a last burst of color before winter sets in. Many plant tulips and daffodils.

Dibble for making holes in the soil

In winter, the earth is at rest. In northern parts of the world, the cold numbs plants, and trees lose their leaves. Only birds and small animals show signs of life. Many gardeners plan what they'll plant in the spring. In moderate climates, gardeners cut off chicory leaves and plant the roots in a dark box. The new leaves that shoot up stay white because they have had no light. This is the vegetable we call endive. It's delicious in green salads.

Garden spade

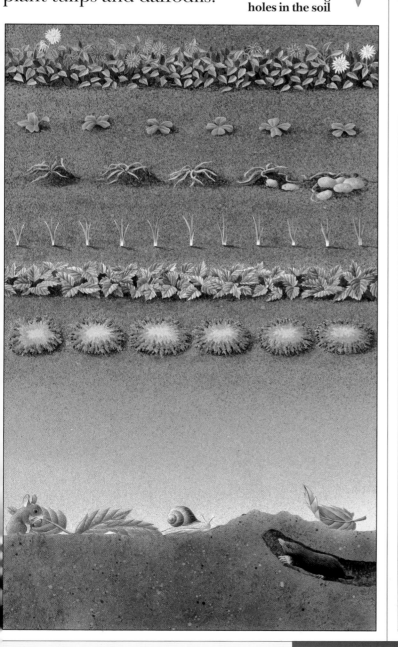

Since prehistoric times people have used animals for food. Early people believed that some of an animal's strength would pass to them if they ate meat from its body.

Paintings found in France's Lascaux Cave are at least 17,000 years old.

Paintings found on the walls of prehistoric caves are often of wild animals such as bison, stags, and bears. Most of the people who lived in these caves were hunters. They used almost every part of the animals they killed: meat, fat, bone, horn, skin, and fur. But they didn't know how to keep food from spoiling, and they risked starvation if the hunting was poor. Gradually, they learned to keep flocks of animals—pigs, sheep, goats, and cattle—and to domesticate them.

Prehistoric people painted animals on the walls of their caves to bring them luck when they went hunting.

All domestic animals have wild ancestors.

Raising animals changed people's lifestyle. They spent more time looking after their herds and growing crops, instead of gathering wild plants for food. Once, they had been nomads, wandering the land. Now groups of people settled in one place and built permanent villages. With their stores of grain and a supply of meat and milk from their flocks, people were less and less dependent on hunting and gathering food from the wild. They started to cut down trees to make larger fields and pastures for their herds.

Some of the different types of meat that come from beef:

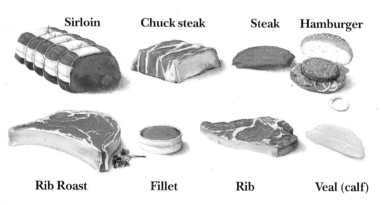

Sirloin   Chuck steak   Steak   Hamburger

Rib Roast   Fillet   Rib   Veal (calf)

People have domesticated animals for more than 6,000 years. Through skillful rearing and crossbreeding, people have improved cows for dairy and beef production. The aurochs, the wild ancestor of the domestic cow, is now extinct. Cattle are not native to the Americas. Early explorers and colonists brought the first cows here. Today, British breeds such as Angus and Hereford are common in the United States.

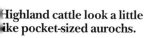

Highland cattle look a little like pocket-sized aurochs.

Simmental (beef and milk)   German Yellow (beef)

West Highland (mainly beef)   Aberdeen Angus (beef)

Normande (milk)   Finn Cattle (milk)

Breton Pie noire (milk)   Meuse Rhein Issel (milk)

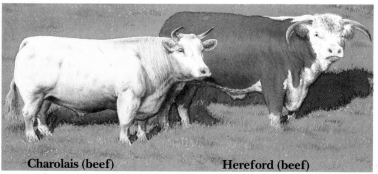

Charolais (beef)   Hereford (beef)

Pigs were the first animals that humans domesticated.

One in three of all the pigs in the world lives in China. For thousands of years, people there have reared them. Pigs have been kept in Europe for a long time too. In the Middle Ages, they roamed the forests in the care of a swineherd, or wandered the streets of the towns. Early settlers in North America imported pigs from England. Today, most pigs live on farms.

Welsh   Tamworth   Danish Landrace

Some of the world's most popular breeds

Pigs like eating and get fat quickly. In the fields or in their pens, pigs snuffle around on the ground with their snouts, feasting on worms and snails, as well as roots and plants. Pigs love rolling in the mud, which helps to keep them cool. Their eyes can't see very far, but they can hear well.

When pigs hear the farmer coming with a bucket of scraps, they snort with excitement. They eat almost anything: potatoes, beets, cereals . . . and they drink more than two gallons (10 l) of water each day.

A sow has a dozen piglets twice a year. She is pregnant for about 114 days before giving birth to her litter. At feeding time, she squeals to her piglets, and they come rushing, knocking each other over as they nuzzle up to her teats.

A sow has 12 teats, and each piglet goes to its own particular one. Clever piglets choose the top teats, which give the most milk. These piglets will grow up to be the strongest in the litter. If there are more than 12 piglets, the farmer must feed the weakest ones from a bottle just as he would a human baby.

Pietrain   Large White   Gloucester Old Spot

Each type of pig is a slightly different shape.

Saddleback   Curly coat   Berkshire

A tightly curled tail is a sign of good health.

Growing quickly in tight places

Many pigs are kept in large feedlots, more like factories than farms. The sows and their litters are kept in special sties, the female pigs in groups, and the male pigs, the boars, separate. Because they live in a tiny pen with hardly any room to move, the pigs get fat more quickly than they would out in a field. Females are forced to give birth more than twice a year.

They are given their meals automatically. If a pig is thirsty, it presses a lever and water runs into a trough. When the pigs weigh about 200 pounds (100 kg), at around five months old, they are taken to the slaughterhouse to be killed.

The meat from a pig is called pork. If it is smoked or cured, it is called ham or bacon. Some religions do not allow their followers to eat pork. Some foods made from pork, pâté or sausages, for example, have a high fat content.

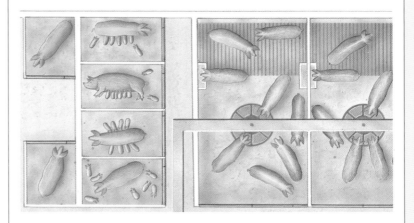

It's better for people's health to cut the fat off chops or ham.

Roast pork, bacon, sausages, ham, chops, and pâté

Salami sausage

Black Pudding

Italian Zampone

Sausages

Ham

Minced pork

Pâté

Smoked Bacon

Cutlets

Pork roast on the bone

and off the bone

Loin chops

Fillet half leg

Fillet

Blade

Hand and spring

Belly

Head

Knuckle

Trotters

How a butcher sees a pig

Pork hocks

Bacon

Blade

On small farms in the past, it was a big day when a pig was killed and the meat prepared for winter storage. One pig could feed a family for a year. Now pigs are usually killed in a slaughterhouse.

In farms all over the world people raise animals.

A female rabbit—called a doe—may have four litters a year. She makes a nest, then plucks the soft fur from her underside to line the inside for her young.

Farm buildings have many uses. The buildings on a farm may be dotted around fields, arranged along a track, or grouped around a farmyard. Each animal needs a shelter, and the farmer and his family need a house to live in too. Cattle have barns; pigs have sties. There may be a barn with pens for the sheep in winter, a chicken coop, and hutches if the farmer keeps rabbits—as well as sheds for the farm machinery, barns for the hay and straw, silos for storing silage, and grain bins for grain.

These three farms are all different, but on each one the farmer grows food for the animals—livestock that in turn supply people with food.

A farm in Britain . . .

. . . another in Africa . . .

. . . and a third in North America, with its tall silo.

Sheep graze on grass in summer, but in winter farmers often feed them hay or root vegetables.

Hens, geese, ducks, turkeys, and chickens . . .

On some farms you might see different birds scratching and pecking at the ground. Hens produce eggs all year long, and chicken is a popular meat. A goose or a turkey may be part of traditional holiday dinners. Roast duck and guinea fowl are delicious. Did you know that geese make good guard dogs? They sound the alarm if a stranger comes near, hissing and honking as loudly as they can!

Hens scratch in the ground and groom themselves by flicking dust through their feathers. They hate getting wet!

Domestic geese stay on the farm; they don't migrate to a warmer climate in winter as their wild cousins do. Have you heard of a gaggle of geese? It is a flock, with a male, or gander, in charge. People can eat goose eggs, and geese are also raised for their meat. People have raised poultry for their eggs and meat since the Chinese began to keep chickens more than 2,000 years ago.

Some of the eggs we eat come from factory farms. Farmers keep the birds cooped up in rows of wire cages in huge barns, with sloping floors for the eggs to roll down. It is a speedy, economical way to farm, but many people feel it is cruel. With so many animals close together, diseases spread easily among the birds. Hens that roam a farmyard are called free-range. Farmers feed them corn, meal, and vegetable scraps, but they like worms and insects too. Free-range hens also peck up tiny pieces of grit to help digest their food and make strong shells for their eggs. The chicken coop is well-lit inside, because light stimulates the hens to lay. In winter, when the days are shorter, hens lay fewer eggs.

A cockerel may rule a roost of eight or 10 hens.

What's in an egg? Inside the shell there is a golden yolk with a transparent, sticky liquid—the white—all around it. When the cock and hen mate, the cock fertilizes the egg. The hen sits on the egg and keeps it warm; a tiny spot on the yolk develops into a chick. The yolk and white are food for the chick until it hatches. The eggs we eat never have a chick inside, because they are not fertilized. A hen whose eggs are taken away sometimes turns broody. The farmer then lets her sit on her newly laid eggs and brood them until they hatch, 21 days later.

A chick hatches. The chick pecks at the shell from inside and cracks it open. When it hatches, the baby bird weighs only one to two ounces (28 to 57 g), the same as a large egg. When its fluffy down dries out, it can walk and scratch for food on its own. By five months old, hens produce their first eggs, and chickens are big enough to be eaten. Both eggs and chicken meat are high in proteins, which help build and repair our muscles.

A sitting hen turns her eggs so that they are all kept equally warm.

Farmers used to raise cattle on every farm. The bullocks would pull the plow, and the cows would provide milk for drinking and for making butter and cheese. The cows also produced a calf each year, which the farmer could fatten and sell at market. The farmers even saved the animals' manure to spread on the fields as fertilizer.

Cows eat grass, but they also like barley, corn, beets, and soybeans.

Cows eat up to 130 pounds (60 kg) of grass a day. In winter, when little pasture is available, they also eat hay, cereals, beets, and soybeans. They drink six large buckets full of water every day.

Chewing the cud, or ruminating

Grass is difficult to digest, but cows have developed a special way of coping. First, they pull up the grass with their rough tongue and swallow it, hardly chewing it at all. The grass goes into the first and largest stomach, to be softened by the juices there. Later, when the cows are resting, the food comes back into their mouth. They chew it once more, slowly and thoroughly, before swallowing it again to be digested in the second stomach. (You can see how this works by following the different colored arrows on the diagram.)

During spring and summer, farmers in mountain areas take their herds up to high meadows, where the grass and clover are sweetest. Often the oldest cow in each herd is the leader.

In winter, most cows stay inside. The barn used to be part of the farmhouse. The heat from the animals' bodies helped to keep the farm family warm.

Dairy farmers produce milk from herds of cows.

During spring and summer, cows graze on open pasture in the mountains.

Today, cows spend the winter in barns that sometimes open out on yards or fields.

Cows are milked every morning and evening. If the farmer is late, the cows get impatient and moo loudly.

When does a cow give milk? When she has a calf. A cow is a mammal, which means she suckles her young with milk. She carries the calf inside her for nine months. As soon as it is born, her udders fill with milk to feed it.

A cow that has not yet had a calf is called a heifer.

A cow has four or five calves in her life, and gives more than 5,250 gallons (20,000 l) of milk. That's enough to fill two big tankers!

For 10 months after her calf is born, a cow produces about five gallons (20 l) of milk a day. She has a calf every year. By the age of six or seven, a cow is too old to have calves and does not give as much milk. Scientists are looking for ways to improve the milk that a cow yields. The type and quality of food she eats is important.

Farmers used to milk cows by hand.

People used to drink milk just as it was, straight from the udder. But tiny bacteria grow in untreated milk, and some of them can make you ill.

In the 19th century, **Louis Pasteur,** a French scientist, discovered a way to destroy these bacteria. He heated the milk to a high temperature for a few seconds, then quickly cooled it down. Today, most milk is treated in this way. The process, called pasteurization (after its inventor), keeps milk fresh for several days.

Bacteria seen under a microscope are much larger than life.

What happens at the dairy?

Most modern farmers use milking machines to help them milk their cows. Machines take only five minutes to milk each cow. The farmer gives her something to eat, so she will stand quietly while the job is done. First the udders are wiped clean. A milking machine sucks out the milk and takes it by pipe to a tank, where it is cooled. The cold keeps bacteria from developing. A refrigerated milk tanker collects the milk each day, sometimes twice a day, and takes it to be processed at the dairy factory.

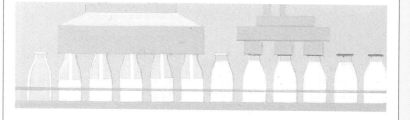

At the dairy, everything must be clean. The amount of cream in the milk is measured, and often some is skimmed off to make 1% and 2% milk. All milk contains important proteins and minerals, such as calcium, which help people's bones and teeth grow strong and healthy.

Milk is made into cream, butter, cheese, and yogurt.

Thousands of years ago, people learned to make cheese when they began to keep dairy animals. Making cheese was a good way to use up old, stale milk. Cheese is made from the curdled milk of cows, sheep, or goats. All over the world, people make different kinds of cheese, each with a different taste and texture. The cream from milk is made into butter.

Separator

Churn

Mold

Cream is the richest part of milk. In this old-fashioned dairy, the farmer and his family are making cream and butter. A separator spins quickly to separate the cream from the milk. Then the cream is tipped into a churn, where it is beaten. It turns yellow and becomes firm as specks of fat in the cream stick together. As the butter forms, a thin liquid called buttermilk runs off of it. It takes more than 10 quarts (9.5 l) of milk to make one pound (0.45 kg) of butter.

Double cream and whipped cream

If salt is added, butter keeps longer. Butter used to be left in pats, or shaped in wooden molds. Today it is wrapped in paper or put into plastic containers.

Butter contains vitamin A, which helps prevent infection and is good for teeth, skin, bones, and eyes. Some doctors and dietitians think that we shouldn't eat too much butter or margarine—they are high in the sort of fats that are unhealthy.

Roquefort, France: sheep's milk

Stilton, England: cow's milk

Feta, Greece: sheep's milk

Edam, Holland: cow's milk

Cheese can be hard, like cheddar, or soft, like brie.

Most American cheeses are made from cow's milk. Each originally came from a different part of the world. A Stilton cheese has blue veins in it, because it is treated with a special mold and left to mature for six to nine months. French cheeses are famous worldwide—there are more than 400 different kinds.

Traditional cheese-making

Different cheeses are made in different ways, but they all start off with curdling.

The milk is warmed, and then starter is added to make the milk sour. Next, rennet, from a calf's stomach, is put in to make the milk clot and set. The milk separates into curds and whey.

Swiss Emmenthal is matured in temperatures between 70° and 80° Fahrenheit (22° and 27°C). Bubbles of carbon dioxide build up inside the cheese, forming holes.

The solid curds are put into a bag so that the liquid whey drains off. Next, hard cheeses have to be pressed. Some, like cheddar, are mixed with salt first. Then they are put in a large mold and pressed together tightly.

Finally, the cheese is left to mature. This is when the flavor of each cheese develops.

Cheddar is usually kept for about five months, but mature cheddar is kept for at least 10 months and has a much stronger taste.

A cellar of maturing cheeses

Sardine   Whiting

Mackerel   Herring

People have been eating fish and shellfish for thousands of years. Scientists have found seashells, fish bones, and fish hooks among ancient rubbish that may be 10,000 years old. Thousands of different kinds of fish live in the sea, and many of them are good to eat. Some live in the open sea; others prefer the shoreline or the seabed. People who fish have to know where each kind lives and feeds so they have a good chance of catching them.

Fishing crews with special boats called trawlers go far out to sea for weeks or months at a time to catch fish. A huge, funnel-shaped net—called a trawl—drags behind the boat. The trawl pulls up cod, sole, and plaice from the ocean bottom. Drift nets that hang in the water like curtains catch herring and mackerel near the ocean surface.

The biggest trawlers are like floating factories. The crew must gut, clean, and freeze the fish on board the ship or the fish will rot.

Fish and shellfish are the harvest of the sea.

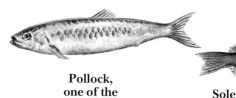

Pollock,
one of the
cod family

Sole

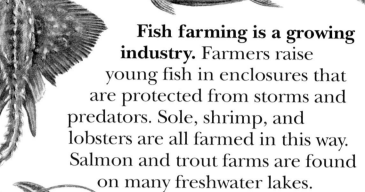

Tuna

Skate

Bass, pollock, and sea bream live close to shore. Fishing crews use a line with hooks all along it to catch them. To catch tuna, crews use boats that carry a boom, a sort of long pole with several fishing lines running from one end of it.

Fish farming is a growing industry. Farmers raise young fish in enclosures that are protected from storms and predators. Sole, shrimp, and lobsters are all farmed in this way. Salmon and trout farms are found on many freshwater lakes.

Crab

Shrimp

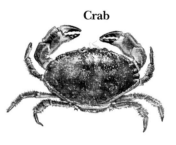

Lobster

Mussels

Periwinkles

Oysters

You can find many interesting things along the seashore at low tide. Beachcombers copy professional fishing crews and use shovels, rakes, and knives to gather shellfish (like clams, scallops, cockles, and periwinkles) that are left behind when the tide goes out.

Some shellfish bury themselves in the sand or mud. Others, such as mussels and limpets, cling to rocks.

For too long people have taken the riches of the sea for granted. Some species are in danger from overfishing.

Laws now control when and where fishing can take place, as well as the amount of fish each country's fishing fleet can take from the sea.

Mussel and oyster farms are now becoming more common. The young larvae are fixed to a suitable rough surface below the tide mark where they can grow in safety.

All fish is good for us, and it's delicious too. It gives us magnesium, phosphorus, vitamins, protein, and oils.

Mussel and oyster farms have been set up along stretches of coast that are exposed at low tide.

Salt is everywhere—in the sea, in the soil, even in the rain. Salt is vital for our health: it helps to regulate how much water our body contains. But where does the salt we eat come from? It is naturally present in many of our foods. The salt we add to food has been extracted from the sea or from underground. Before refrigerators, people used salt to preserve food. Salted meat keeps for a long time.

People have collected salt from the sea ever since ancient times. The Romans were the first to build salt pans. Seawater circulated slowly along channels through a series of shallow pools. The sun's heat made the water evaporate, and the salt was left behind.

When the salt forms crystals, the salt-maker collects it in a pile and pushes it toward the dike. The large, gray crystals fall to the bottom, leaving the tiny, white crystals gleaming on top.

In other African countries, such as Mali, people cut the salty crust on the ground into blocks, which they pry up with long sticks. The people shape the blocks into slabs, and camels carry the slabs to the nearest market. Salt is precious to animals and people who live in the desert. Eating salt helps their bodies replace the salt they lose through sweating in the heat.

Salt was once an expensive commodity. It could be exchanged for slaves or gold, and there were even coins made of salt. Roman soldiers were paid partly in salt, and now when people talk of earning a "salary," they are using a word that comes from the Latin word for salt.

In some African deserts, salt lakes come and go with the rainy and dry seasons, year after year. When the lakes evaporate, they leave a crust of salt over the land.

In Niger the ground is full of salt, and the spring water that collects in natural basins is salty too. The local people collect the salt and pour it into molds made from the hollowed-out trunks of palm trees. When the water evaporates, the people break the molds and are left with loaves of salt.

An open-cast salt mine in Mali. Salt is cut into slabs, each weighing about 130 pounds (60 kg), and then camels take them to market.

The salt that miners dug up from mines was left behind by the oceans that once covered the planet millions of years ago.

The first salt miners

Each time the Earth's crust shifted, the salt was buried deeper under rock and soil. People dug the first salt mines about 3,000 years ago. For people living far from the sea, salt mines were a great discovery. Miners went down into the mines on ropes, used picks to dig out huge blocks of salt, and carried them up on their backs. Later, the miners used horses to bring the salt up in barrels.

Miners used picks with heads made of bronze. Oil lamps hanging from the walls lit up the mines.

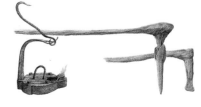

People discovered the many uses of salt a long time ago. Meat and fish steeped in salt keep for several months, because salt absorbs the water in food and dries it out. Salt also destroys the bacteria that make food rot.

For a healthy diet, nutritionists say we should avoid salty foods and not add too much salt to our food.

Now almost every country in the world, except the Scandinavian countries and Japan, produces its own salt. Most of the salt is rock salt that miners dig out of mines. The largest producers in the world are the United States and China.

Ancient Egyptians plucked and dressed ducks they had killed, then packed them in salt.

The Scandinavian countries of northern Europe had no salt mines and not enough sunshine to evaporate the water in salt pans. They had to buy salt from France, Italy, and Portugal, and pay for it in gold. The salt came by boat over the sea and up the rivers, and then overland on mules. The salt trade was valued; at times wars were waged over it.

In a modern mine, salt is extracted on a massive scale. One explosion can bring down 550 tons (500,000 kg) of salt. Miners load the pieces onto bulldozers that carry them off to a machine that breaks and crushes them. Other machines wash the salt, separate it, and put it into packets.

People used salt as a medicine.

A spoonful of sweet, sticky honey tastes great on bread. For thousands of years, people have enjoyed eating honey. They learned to look for it in the hollow trees where wild bees nest. Beekeepers keep bees in small wooden houses called beehives so they can collect the honey easily. Thousands of bees may live in one hive. Most of them are females, and each has a job to do.

| Lime | Acacia | Chestnut | Fir | Thyme |

Bees produce honey of different flavors using different flowers.

There is one queen in each hive. She lays eggs that hatch into white larvae and then turn into young bees. A few bees are drones—male bees whose job is to fertilize the queen. All the others are female workers. They look after the larvae, clean the hive, and collect nectar and pollen from the flowers to make wax and honey.

A worker bee's body has special tools. Its long tongue sucks up nectar from flowers. The hairs on its back legs collect the pollen. Its strong upper jaws, or mandibles, soften the wax and build cells where the larvae are cared for and where the honey is kept.

Bees attach the pollen to sacs on their back legs.

Bees make honey from nectar. In the hive, worker bees turn the sugary liquid into a sticky paste by beating their wings over it. Then they chew it up. Some is mixed with pollen to feed the larvae. The rest is stored in cells that are plugged shut with wax. This is the honey that the beekeeper collects.

Beekeepers take the roof off the hive and lift out the frames of honey. They scrape off the top covering of wax, then spin it in a machine called a separator to make the honey run out. In a single season, one beekeeper may collect 35 large jars full of honey. But beekeepers always leave enough for the bees to live on through the winter.

Every green plant has chlorophyll in its cells—it's what makes the leaves green. Chlorophyll absorbs the sun's rays and combines them with water and carbon dioxide gas in the air to make sugar. A plant stores sugar in its fruit, sap, stalk, roots, and leaves.

Sugar cane is particularly rich in sugar.

This kind of reed grows in tropical countries, where the climate is hot and humid. Inside the sugar cane is a firm, white pulp where the sugar is stored. It is deliciously sweet and juicy to chew on.

Planting sugar cane

Short sections of sugar cane, called sets, are planted in trenches.

They take root and send up a shoot. Eighteen months later, the canes are cut. Every year for five or six years, fresh canes are cut from the old ones. Then it is time to plant new sets.

Harvesting the cane

When the canes are about 15 feet (5 m) high, they are ready to be cut. Today machines often harvest the cane.

The brown juice is boiled, and dirt and impurities are removed. The juice thickens as the water evaporates.

After awhile, sugar crystals begin to appear. Brown sugar crystals are turned into white ones in a refinery, where the crystals are melted down and cleaned again. The whiter the sugar, the more refined it is.

Sugar was once expensive in many parts of the world, such as Europe, because it had to be shipped in from far away.

In many places people cut the canes by hand using a long knife called a machete. It's hard work. Workers pick up the cut cane, and they have to transport it to the sugar factory as quickly as possible. As soon as canes are cut, they begin to lose their sweetness.

The sugar mill

Canes used to be crushed in a mill. As the mill ground down the canes, a dark brown liquid full of bits of leaf and stem was squeezed out. Now, in most parts of the world, modern factories use machines to grind the canes and make the juice, which is collected in vats and heated.

Sugar used to be poured into cone-shaped molds while it was still hot.

Sugar was once a luxury.

From the 18th century onward, chocolate and coffee became popular in Europe—and people demanded sugar to sweeten them. In 1807, England was at war with France, and all overseas trade came to a standstill. Ports were blocked, and the ships bringing sugar cane were not allowed to get through.

The English had developed a sweet tooth, and so had the French. How would they get sugar now?

The answer was in the ground: sugar beets, a vegetable that grows well in mild climates. As it grows, this plant stores sugar in its thick, white root.

People had been experimenting with carrots, grapes, and even potatoes, to see which would produce the most sugar. The best results came from sugar beets. In 1802, French chemist Benjamin Delessert discovered a way of extracting the sugar from sugar beets.

Emperor Napoleon of France was pleased and ordered huge fields of sugar beets to be planted. Soon the French had lots of sugar. Today, sugar beets are a major crop in the United States too.

Farmers plant sugar beet seeds in the spring. By May, clumps of green leaves appear above the ground. In the warmth of the summer sun, sugar begins to collect in the root as it grows larger.

All through the fall, farmers harvest the beets. Machines cut off the leaves and haul the beets out of the ground. Workers take the harvested beets to a factory, where machines extract the sugar.

During the harvest, people in the factories work day and night. In the U.S., almost half of the sugar crop comes from sugar beets; the rest comes from sugar cane either grown in Hawaii or imported from tropical countries.

Three hundred years ago, sugar was a luxury, an expensive treat kept for special occasions. Today, you can find it in many foods, from baked beans to yogurt.

Sweet things like candy, ice cream, and soda pop are made with large amounts of sugar. If you're playing, sugar can give you a quick burst of energy when you're tired. But too much sugar causes cavities in your teeth and is stored in your body as fat.

Granulated sugar, which is made up of tiny crystals, can be shaped into sugar cubes, ground into white sugar that you sprinkle on your cereal, or ground even more finely into powdered sugar. Sugar candy is made of larger crystals, which take longer to form.

You can eat it, mix it with milk and drink it, make ice cream with it—but just what is chocolate? It comes from the beans of the cocoa tree, a plant that flowers all year round. The flowers ripen into pods, and inside each one are 30 or 40 seeds, wrapped in a soft white pulp. These are cocoa beans.

The flowers of the cocoa tree grow straight out of the trunk and main branches and ripen into pods.

Cocoa trees like hot, damp climates.

They are grown throughout the tropical regions of Africa and South America. When they grow wild in the forest, they can be 30 to 50 feet (10 to 15 m) high, but in plantations, they are cut back to keep them about 15 feet (5 m) high, to make it easier to harvest the pods.

When they are ripe, the pods are a beautiful red or orange color. Workers pick them and slice them in half, then take the beans out of the white pulp.

Who first tried chocolate as a drink?

The recipe comes from Mexico, where the Aztecs, the local Indians, drank it. The first European to taste it was the Spanish general Hernán Cortés in the 16th century. The Aztec emperor Montezuma welcomed him with a present of cocoa pods and offered him a drink made from cocoa beans.

The Aztecs of Mexico grilled the cocoa beans, then crushed and mixed them with maize flour, pepper, vanilla, and water. It made a nourishing, but rather bitter, drink. Cortés liked it so much that he sent a boat back to Spain packed entirely with cocoa beans.

The Aztecs used the dried beans for trading—10 cocoa beans might buy a rabbit.

Cooks at the Spanish court thought the drink should be less bitter, so they added sugar to it instead of pepper. What a success! The new drink became most fashionable among the rich and elegant, and every noble lord wanted a chocolate-maker as part of his household.

The fashion of drinking chocolate spread across Europe. Doctors recommended it to their patients as a tonic. Then in the 19th century, Meunier, Lindt, Fry, and Cadbury were among the first chocolate manufacturers to make blocks of chocolate in their factories.

Fresh cocoa beans taste bitter—not at all like chocolate.

How are cocoa beans made to taste like chocolate? Once they have been picked out of their pulp, they are left for a week in large chests, covered with damp banana leaves. Every day, workers stir them. The beans ferment and turn brown, taking on their special taste.

Once they ferment, workers spread out the beans on large trays to dry in the sun for a week or two. The workers regularly turn over the beans to make sure they dry out evenly. If it rains, the workers use runners to slide the trays back under cover. If the beans crack when workers squeeze them, they are thoroughly dry and will keep for a long time without getting moldy. Now they are ready to be packed into sacks and put on board ships for export to other countries.

Cocoa beans have a long journey before they reach the chocolate factories. Cocoa is grown in Cameroon, Ecuador, Ghana, Nigeria, Brazil, and the Ivory Coast. Cocoa is a cash crop that is exported to Europe and North America, where the beans are made into chocolate for use in many products.

Cocoa trees grow in countries with tropical climates, mainly in West Africa, South America, Asia, and Malaysia.

In the chocolate factory, the beans are first sorted and cleaned. Then they are grilled to crack open the shells and bring out their full flavor. Machines crush them into a bitter paste, which is pressed hard to squeeze out all the fat. This is called cocoa butter. To make chocolate, the cocoa paste, cocoa butter, and sugar are mixed together and stirred for two or three days without stopping. Later, dried milk powder, raisins, nuts, or puffed grains of rice can be added to make different kinds of chocolate products.

The story goes that shepherds in Yemen were the discoverers of coffee. They noticed that their goats became lively after eating the red berries from a particular bush, so the shepherds tried the berries themselves and found they could not sleep at night. The plant was a coffee bush.

A ripe coffee berry looks like a small red cherry. Inside are two green beans, which turn brown once they are roasted.

Large coffee plantations

Today, coffee is grown in most tropical countries, especially in Africa and South America. The largest coffee crops come from Brazil.

Until the 19th century, slaves brought from Africa worked on some of the plantations. They looked after the coffee plants, watered the bushes, and picked the ripened berries.

Coffee is a sensitive plant. Too much or too little rain or cold temperatures can destroy a whole crop.

Harvesting coffee

When the berries are ripe, workers pick them by hand, one by one, or pull them off the bushes using special combs. Once gathered into baskets, the berries are dried and boiled to release the beans.

Green coffee beans don't have a smell. They become brown and begin to have the coffee smell that you recognize only after they've been roasted.

Each kind of coffee has a different flavor. Arabica, from Brazil and Colombia, is the most popular. African Robusta has a more bitter taste.

Like coffee, tea contains a chemical called caffeine, which can make the drinker feel energetic. Tea also comes from a plant that grows in hot climates. The Chinese first noticed that tea leaves steeped in boiling water made a delicious drink. Drinking tea also has been a custom in Japan for thousands of years; people there have developed a special tea ceremony.

Dutch merchants traveled to Japan and brought tea back to Europe in the 16th century. It became popular in Europe, especially in Britain. Colonists brought tea to America. When the British put a tax on the tea it shipped to them, the colonists dumped the tea into the harbor in protest of the tax. This was the Boston Tea Party, one of the events that led to the American Revolution.

Tea leaves are picked by hand, one by one. The best tea is made from pekoe: the youngest, most tender leaves growing at the tip of the stem.

The next four or five leaves along the stalk are worth picking too, but the others are all too tough. Workers harvest the tea leaves all year long. The leaves are spread out, dried, turned, and heated. Gradually they turn brown. Sometimes tea leaves are flavored with flowers such as jasmine.

Herbs and spices add exciting flavors to food.

Have you ever walked into a kitchen and sniffed the peppery smell of gingerbread baking in the oven? Ginger is a spice that can make your nose twitch. The jars of brownish powder labeled cinnamon, ginger, and nutmeg may look unexciting, but the spices they contain add strong, warming flavors to food. Herbs also give extra taste to food. Each has its own smell and flavor. Herbs may be used fresh or dried. People sometimes cook their food in oil or use it in a dressing. Oil is a rich, clear liquid that comes from plants.

Most of the spices we use come from the East.

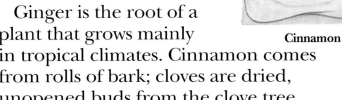

Cinnamon

One of the first spices people used was pepper. It came from India.

Ginger is the root of a plant that grows mainly in tropical climates. Cinnamon comes from rolls of bark; cloves are dried, unopened buds from the clove tree.

For hundreds of years, these spices, along with nutmeg and sesame seeds, were rare and expensive products. During the Middle Ages, only rich nobles could afford them. It was not easy to keep food fresh, and the strong flavor of spices helped disguise the taste of stale meat and fish. Many spices were also used as medicines.

Some common spices:

A stem from a pepper plant shows its seeds, the peppercorns.

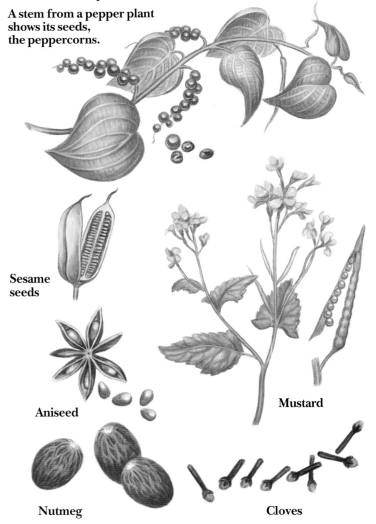

Sesame seeds

Aniseed

Mustard

Nutmeg

Cloves

Fresh herbs

Rosemary

Sorrel

Mint

Parsley

Chives

Tarragon

Olives are the fruit of the olive tree.

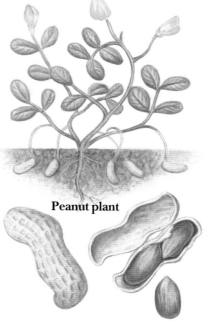

Peanut plant

Peanuts are the seeds.

Next, the seeds go through a press that reduces them to a pulp and releases their oil, which at this stage is thick. The oil must be refined and distilled to make it easier for people to digest.

You can grow herbs in a garden or in a pot on the windowsill. A few sprigs of thyme, rosemary, basil, or a bay leaf add delicious flavors to soup, fish, or meat. Parsley, chives, and tarragon can be finely chopped and sprinkled on salads and other dishes. Cooks have been using all these herbs since the Middle Ages. Like spices, they can also be used as medicines.

Some plants give us oil. It is made from the crushed seeds of certain plants. Some, such as cotton, soybeans, and peanuts, need hot temperatures to grow. Others, like rape, sunflowers, or corn grow in cooler countries. Coconuts and olives also give oil.

How is the oil produced? The outer husks are removed, then the seeds are crushed and heated gently to get rid of excess water.

Ounce for ounce, oil contains more calories than any other food. Oil gives us energy as well as many of the minerals and vitamins we need to grow. Sunflower, peanut, and soybean oil are used to make margarine. It can be used in place of butter althought it has a different taste.

Rape

Sunflowers are laden with seeds. They turn their heads to face the sun—which is how the plant got its name. New strains have been developed, though, that don't turn toward the sun.

Intriguing facts,
activities, games,
a quiz, and a glossary,
followed by the index

In many countries, people bake bread for special occasions. Bread can be crisp like a biscuit or soft and spongy.

Chinese New Year bread **German New Year's Pretzel**

Easter Plait **Pilgrim's bread**

The croissant is a soft, flaky bread made in the shape of a crescent. It was first made in 1683 in Vienna, Austria. Turks had besieged the city, but their army was beaten and they fled, leaving behind large stocks of coffee. A Polish man opened a cafe, and he asked a baker to make something to serve with the coffee. To commemorate the victory, the baker made bread shaped like the crescent on the Turkish flag.

French bread goes into space! In 1985 special sticks of French bread were made for the astronauts to take with them on the space shuttle Columbia. The bread was special because it didn't make any crumbs.

In many countries around the Mediterranean, a sweet bread almost like a cake is made at Easter. It is decorated with a red painted egg.

In parts of what used to be called Yugoslavia, if a boy is in love with a girl, he gives her a little heart made of bread.

Every country, every region, bakes its own type of bread. Have you ever seen these breads?

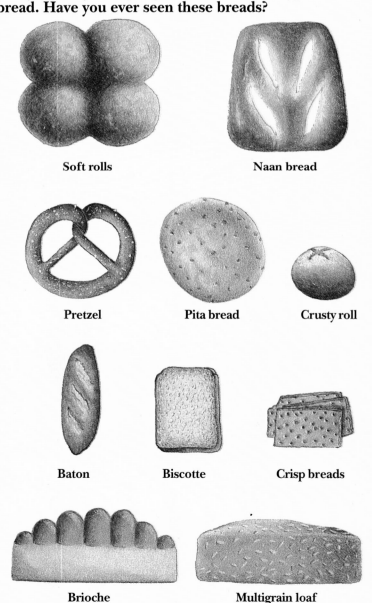

Soft rolls **Naan bread**

Pretzel **Pita bread** **Crusty roll**

Baton **Biscotte** **Crisp breads**

Brioche **Multigrain loaf**

Pasta was invented by the Chinese. In 1271, Marco Polo set out from Venice to explore the East. For 24 years he traveled in China, Mongolia, and India. When he returned home, he brought back the recipe for pasta. Now, pasta is one of the specialties of Italian cooking.

Sandwiches were the invention of John Montagu, fourth Earl of Sandwich, who was a very keen card player. One day in 1762, he was so involved in a game that he refused to stop for dinner. He asked for a slice of meat between two pieces of bread. It was the very first sandwich.

Canned food was the brainstorm of Parisian Nicolas Appert. The French government was offering a prize to anyone who could find a way of preserving food for the troops when they were away on a long campaign.

Appert perfected a method of sterilization. He sealed the food in a glass jar, and then heated it to a high temperature—212° Fahrenheit (100°C)—to destroy any bacteria. The experiment was a success. In 1810, Appert won the government's prize.

■ Did you know?

The creamiest type of milk is whole milk. None of the cream has been removed, and if it hasn't been treated, a layer of cream will rise to the top. Semi-skimmed (1% and 2%) milk has had some cream removed, and skimmed milk contains virtually no cream. Unpasteurized milk comes straight from the farm. If it is boiled for 10 minutes, it will keep for a few days in the refrigerator.

Fresh pasteurized milk shows a sell-by date. It will keep, unopened, for several days in the refrigerator. American scientists are testing ways to sterilize liquids at a lower temperature than Pasteur did, because high heat can rob foods of some of their taste and nutrients such as vitamin C.

Apicius, a Roman citizen who lived in the 1st century B.C., wrote the first cookbook. He wrote down the ingredients for each recipe, but not their quantities. He invented dishes using such delicacies as larks' and flamingos' tongues, camels' fetlocks, and sows' udders. He also gave several recipes for cakes and sauces.

Besides cows' milk, people also drink goats' milk, sheep's milk, and in certain countries, milk from horses, donkeys, and camels.

Buffalo   **Female zebu**

In Asia, Tibetans drink yak's milk.

The Lapps in Finland, Sweden, and Norway drink the milk from the herds of reindeer they follow.

The Tuareg people of Africa move their herds from place to place to find grazing for their animals.

The Indians of the Andes Mountains drink llamas' milk.

Plates

Many people used to help themselves and eat straight from the main cooking pot. Then in the Middle Ages the porringer appeared—it was an individual bowl for soup. People ate bread and meat from thick pieces of wood called trenchers. Although rich people used them sooner, plates were not common until the end of the 18th century.

Knives

Right up to the end of the 16th century, people had their own knives, which they took with them if they went to dine with a friend. These knives had sharp points for spearing and serving the meat.

Forks

For a long time, people ate with their fingers—which is still the practice in some cultures. By the Middle Ages, the nobility in Europe used forks, which were a luxury. Forks did not become widely used until the end of the 18th century.

Glasses

People used to drink from cups that were like small bowls with handles. These cups were made from clay, wood, metal, or carved stone.

■ Did you know?

Snails have long been considered a delicacy. The Romans fattened them on snail farms. In the Middle Ages, snails were fried with onions. The French still cook dishes with snails.

Pigs hunt for truffles. A truffle is a type of mushroom with a strong smell. Truffles grow underground, mostly under oak trees. Farmers use sows, with their fine sense of smell, to root in the earth and uncover truffles. Pâté flavored with truffles is a luxury.

Pigs can be pets! In Papua New Guinea, a large island to the north of Australia, people treat young pigs as pets. The pigs live in the house with the family; owners take them for walks on leashes. The more pigs a family owns, the richer it is considered to be. Unfortunately for the pig, when it is fully grown it is killed and eaten at a large feast.

■ Quiz

Choose the correct answer to each question—you'll find the answers on page 67.

1. What is Roquefort cheese made from?
a. sheep's milk
b. cows' milk
c. goats' milk

2. What is pekoe?
a. a fruit
b. the youngest tea leaves
c. a type of fabric

3. What is couscous made from?
a. ground-up corn
b. ground-up rice
c. ground-up wheat

Rice is important in Asia. When farmers on the island of Bali, in Indonesia, pray for a good harvest, they offer beautiful and intricately decorated rice cakes to their gods.

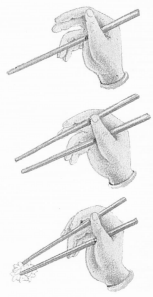

How do you eat with chopsticks? Hold the lower chopstick steady between your thumb and third finger. The top chopstick, held between the tip of your thumb and your index finger, picks up the rice and presses it against the lower chopstick. Rice that sticks together after it has been cooked is easier to pick up.

■ Did you know?

The Hindus in India first discovered sugar. They found a way of making sugar crystals from the juice of a wild cane.

The English word "sugar" comes from the Sanskrit word *sarkara*, meaning sugar crystals. Alexander the Great, king of Macedonia, discovered wild sugar cane on an expedition to India in the 4th century B.C.

The Greeks then began to import sugar. Merchants brought sugar back to northern Europe in the 11th century.

In the United States, an average person eats more than 100 pounds (45 kg) of sugar per year. One hundred years ago, sugar was rare and expensive. A piece of candy was a special treat.

■ Quiz

4. Each day, you should drink at least
a. 3 glasses of water
b. 10 glasses of water
c. 25 glasses of water

5. Which of these would be the best breakfast?
a. a glass of cola and candy
b. sausages, a slice of white toast, and a cup of coffee
c. cereal or whole wheat toast, fruit juice, and yogurt

6. What are vitamins?
a. foods high in calories
b. tiny particles found in water
c. elements in food that are essential for good health

Answers: 1a, 2b, 3c, 4b, 5c, 6c.

There's more to salt than flavoring food! People used to think salt had miraculous healing powers. Ancient Greeks and Romans sprinkled salt on houses to ward off illness. Whether as an ointment, powder, or tonic, doctors would prescribe salt to ease all kinds of aches and pains: wasp stings, heart pain, tooth decay, coughs, and even laziness. Doctors used to wrap up sprains and pulled muscles with poultices made of nettles mixed with salt.

Salt shaker   **Salt box**

Today, people still use salt as a remedy for some ailments. If your feet ache or are swollen, try soaking them in salt water. If your throat feels sore, gargle with warm salt water. If you feel tired, a hot bath with salt in it may help you to relax. But be careful! Doctors think that eating too much salt as an adult can make your blood pressure rise and put strain on your heart.

In winter, trucks spread salt on roads to help melt snow and ice.

■ Marzipan creatures

You'll need:

1 ⅛ cups powdered sugar
1 ⅛ cups ground almonds
2 egg whites
red, green, and yellow food
coloring

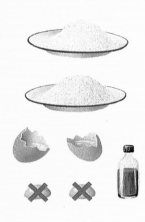

Mix together the
powdered sugar and
ground almonds in a bowl.

Add the egg whites and
mix again into a firm paste
that is easy to work with.
Divide the paste into three
or four balls and mix a few
drops of food coloring
into each one.

To make the animals pictured below, you'll need: pitted
prunes and dates, candied cherries or candy corn,
almonds, walnuts, hazelnuts, raisins or candy chips,
and a few sticks of black licorice.

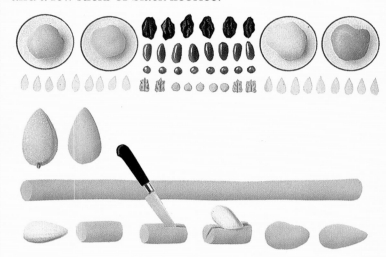

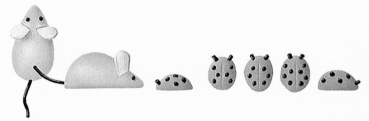

Marzipan mice: Roll a piece of marzipan into a sausage
shape and cut it into pieces, each one a little bigger than
an almond. Split each piece down the middle with a
knife and push an almond inside; then mold the
marzipan around the nut in the shape of a mouse's body.
Use two almonds for ears and licorice pieces for the eyes
and the tail.

Ladybugs: wrap a piece of marzipan around a hazelnut
to create the body; use pieces of licorice to make the
spots and antennae.

Owls: Use pieces of marzipan to model the owl's head
and body. Take a date and split it in two to make the
wings. Use a candied cherry or candy corn for the beak,
licorice for the eyes and ear tufts, and raisins for the feet.

Snails: Roll a piece of marzipan and put a walnut on top
for the body and shell. Use licorice for the antennae.

Use your imagination! Make a butterfly using dates split
in half for the wings, or a porcupine from a ball of
marzipan studded with licorice pieces.

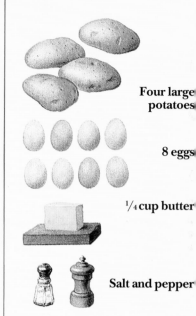

Four large
potatoes

8 eggs

¼ cup butter

Salt and pepper

Eggs in their nests

You'll also need aluminum
foil and an adult to help
you with the oven.
1. Collect the ingredients.
2. Set the oven to 400°
Fahrenheit (200°C).
3. Scrub the potatoes and
wrap each one in
aluminum foil.
4. Bake the potatoes in the
oven for 90 minutes.
5. Slowly melt the butter in
a saucepan.
6. While the potatoes are
still hot, cut them in half
and scoop out the center
of each to make a nest.
7. Lay the halves in a
baking dish. Pour butter
into each nest and break
an egg into it.
8. Sprinkle with salt and
pepper, then put the dish
back in the oven until the
eggs are cooked.

■ Potato prints

You can make wonderful prints using ordinary potatoes. Here's how!

ABCD

First, gather the things you'll need.

To make the stamps:
a few potatoes
a knife with a sharp point—
ask an adult to help you
a pencil

And for the printing:
tubes of paint or a bottle of ink
a small, shallow dish or lid
blotting paper or paper towel
sheets of paper on which to print
newspapers to cover the table
an apron to protect you

You could print a frieze to decorate your writing paper or invitations to your birthday party.

First, make the stamps:
1. Cut a potato in half.
2. Draw a simple, clear design on it, then cut around the design with a knife. The design should stand out in relief. Remember to make any letters backward.

To print:
3. Put a pad of blotting paper or paper towel in the dish or lid, and soak it thoroughly with ink or paint.
4. Press the potato face down onto the pad, then onto a sheet of paper.

Radish seeds   **Compost**

Pebbles

■ Radishes in pots!

Put a few pebbles into a pot; add some compost. Plant three or four radish seeds. Lightly cover them

with compost and water well. Place the pot on a sunny windowsill. Water it every other day. After about a month, your radishes will be ready to eat!

If you're growing the long type of radish, make sure you plant the seeds deep enough so that the radishes don't grow twisted.

Additive: anything that is added to food. Additives can be substances that add color to or improve the flavor of food, or they can be preservatives, which help the food stay fresh longer. Labels on food packaging tell you which additives are in the food.

Aztecs: an American Indian people who settled in what is now Mexico. During the 14th century, they built a powerful and sophisticated empire. They were conquered by the Spanish after 1521.

Bacteria: microscopic organisms found almost everywhere. Some are harmful and cause disease. Others perform useful functions in a healthy body, helping to break down waste products. Bacteria are essential in many food processes, such as the making of butter, cheese, or yogurt.

Bullock: a young bull or one that is no longer capable of breeding.

Calcium: an essential mineral that bodies need to build strong bones and teeth.

Carbohydrate: a compound of carbon, hydrogen, and oxygen that produces energy and is found in food. Sugar and starch are carbohydrates.

Cash crop: a crop grown for sale rather than for the farmer's own use.

Using a pig to search for truffles

Corn dolly: a small decoration made of dried corn stalks with the ear of the grain still intact. They are often intricately woven, and used to be hung around the farmhouse to bring good luck.

Cultivate: to develop a plant using farming or gardening techniques.

Digestion: the process by which human and animal bodies break down food and release its energy and nutrients.

Domesticate: to tame. Pigs, cows, sheep, and goats were once wild animals that people domesticated over the centuries. People first domesticated horses 4,000 years ago.

Fat: a vital source of vitamins and energy. Eating too many saturated fats in meats and dairy products is unhealthy; vegetable fats are better for your body.

Fermentation: bacteria and yeast break down the sugars in food. The process is used in baking bread and in producing cheese, yogurt, and wine.

Fertilizer: anything added to soil—such as animal manure or chemical fertilizers—to help plants grow better.

Fiber: essential to healthy digestion, fiber is in many unprocessed foods and in all fruits and vegetables.

Germination: This takes place when a seed begins to grow. A root goes down into the soil and a shoot goes up.

Harrow: a heavy frame with iron teeth, pulled behind a tractor. It breaks up clods of dirt on plowed land or covers the seeds after sowing.

Incas: South American Indian people of Peru whose empire was at its height in the 15th century.

Their emperor was known as the Inca, and people believed he was descended from their sun god. The Inca civilization was destroyed by the Spanish in the 1530s.

Litter: a brood of young animals born to one mother at the same time.

Migration: some animals, birds, fish, and even insects make long and difficult journeys in search of food or to avoid cold and wet seasons. These seasonal journeys, which happen year after year, are called migration.

Mineral: an inorganic substance such as iron, calcium, or phosphorus that bodies need for healthy growth.

Nectar: a sugary liquid that flowers produce. As insects drink it, they pick up pollen and carry it from one plant to another so flowers are fertilized.

Pollen: a powder flowers produce; pollen plays a part in plant reproduction.

Protein: an essential nutrient in the food of all animals.
Prune: to trim or cut back a plant or encourage vigorous, healthy growth. Growers regularly prune fruit trees so they will produce plenty of fruit.

Seed drill: a machine pulled behind a tractor and used for sowing seeds. The seeds run out of a hopper and down through tubes into the furrows, which are made by a set of blades attached in front. A harrow is drawn along

behind to cover the planted seeds with soil.
Staple food: the basic food eaten in various forms by the people of a particular area. A staple food in Italy is pasta; a staple food in China is rice.

Vegetarian: a person who does not eat meat or fish for reasons of health, principles, or religion. Vegans eat no animal products at all and often do not wear leather.
Vitamins: substances found in foods, especially when raw, which are vital for health and well-being. A diet lacking in vitamins can result in serious diseases such as scurvy or in malnutrition.

Yeast: a yellowish, foamy substance that produces alcohol when in contact with sugar. It is used in wine-making and beer-brewing and it also causes bread to rise.

■ Have you heard these expressions?

Bread
"The bread winner"
The wage earner in a family
"Those items will sell like hot cakes."
Those will sell fast.

Eggs
"He's a good egg."
He's all right—he's a decent person.
"Don't teach your grandmother to suck eggs."
Don't presume to advise someone who is more experienced than you are.

Fruit and vegetables
"You are the apple of her eye."
You're her favorite.
"She had two bites at the cherry."
She had a second chance at trying something.
"That's a hot potato."
That's a touchy subject.
"You know your onions."
You know your job, or your subject, well.

Cheese
"His project is cheesy."
His project was not done well or with care.
"She's a big cheese."
She's important.

Milk
"There's no use crying over spilt milk."
There's no point in moaning about a mistake after the damage has been done.

Fish
"A fish out of water"
A person in an unsuitable or unaccustomed situation
"I have other fish to fry."
I have other business to attend to.
"A red herring."
A subject introduced to divert attention. (A red herring is literally a dried herring with a strong smell. During a hunt, people would drag a dried herring across a trail to put hounds off the scent.)

Animals
"You'll have to wait till the cows come home."
You'll have to wait for a long time.
"I could eat a horse."
I am very hungry.
"A pig in a poke"
An object bought as a bargain
"You've got a bee in your bonnet."
You are obsessed with a particular idea.

"I think you're the bee's knees."
I think you're very special.
"Don't count your chickens before they're hatched."
Don't depend too much on something that hasn't happened yet.
"It's lovely weather for ducks."
It's very wet.
"To take the bull by the horns"
Try to find a solution to a problem without hesitating
"A bull in a china shop"
An insensitive person in a delicate situation

Salt
"I should take it with a grain of salt."
I shouldn't believe every word of that.
"To rub salt in a wound"
To make a bad situation even worse, usually by saying the wrong thing

Tea
"That's not my cup of tea."
That's not the sort of thing I like.
"I wouldn't do that for all the tea in China."
Nothing would make me do that.

General sayings
"Too many cooks in the kitchen spoil the broth."
Too many people trying to do the same job get in each other's way.
"You've bitten off more than you can chew."
You've taken on something that's too much for you to cope with.
"Hunger is the best sauce."
When you're hungry, almost any food tastes delicious.
"Eat your heart out."
Pine away.
"Eat your words."
Take back what you said.
"To reap what you sow"
Get back from life or work what you put into it
"To have all four feet in the trough"
To be completely involved in eating
"To be on the bread line"
Poor (having only enough money to buy food)
"To put something on the back burner"
To rest an idea for awhile and come back to it later
"What's cooking?"
What's going on?

A BALANCED DIET

What we need

Proteins
Muscles, skin, and hair are made of proteins. Cells need proteins to grow and repair themselves.

Carbohydrates provide energy, which is measured in calories.

Fiber is a special type of carbohydrate that is necessary for healthy digestion.

Fats and oils contain vitamins, which allow bodies to store energy, make cell walls, and help our nervous and hormone systems to work well. They also protect organs.

Minerals are vital for healthy bones, teeth, and blood. They help to contract and relax our muscles. They help to regulate the balance of fluid in the body.

Vitamins, like minerals, are essential for growth and well-being.

Eating a balanced diet gives a body everything it needs.

What is a balanced diet?
It is a range of healthy foods eaten in the right variety and in sensible quantities.

The foods you eat provide your body with proteins, carbohydrates, fiber, fats, oils, minerals, and vitamins. These nutrients are essential to the body.

All of these nutrients, in their different ways, provide energy and help to build, maintain, and protect your body. When you are healthy you feel well as you work and play, run and rest.

You are what you eat!
Eating a good balanced diet gives your body every chance to keep fit and healthy. Even simple meals like sandwiches can be varied and wholesome.

To find out more about diet and health, ask a librarian for books on the subject, or ask your family's doctor.

Where you can find what you need:

Beans: protein, carbohydrate, fiber, minerals, vitamins

Bread: carbohydrate, fiber, minerals, vitamins

Eggs: protein, minerals, vitamins

Fish: protein, oils, minerals, vitamins

Fresh vegetables and fruit: fiber, minerals, vitamins

Granola and whole-grain cereals: carbohydrate, fiber, minerals, vitamins

Margarine and oils: oil, vitamins

Meat: protein, fat, minerals, vitamins

Milk, butter, yogurt, cheese: protein, fats, minerals, vitamins

Nuts and seeds: protein, oils, minerals, vitamins

Pasta: carbohydrate

Potatoes: carbohydrate, minerals, vitamins

Rice: carbohydrate, protein, minerals, vitamins

Great food for a party, but not for our everyday balanced diet!

The entries in **bold** refer to whole chapters on the subject.